THE JOURNEY TO PERFECT PEACE

How to Break Free from Overwhelm and Create a Life of Gratitude and Lasting Peace.

Yahreema G McFarlane

Copyright © 2025 by Yahreema G McFarlane

All rights are reserved, and no part of this publication may be reproduced, distributed, or transmitted in any manner, whether through photocopying, recording, or any other electronic or mechanical methods, without the explicit prior written permission of the publisher. This restriction applies to any form or means of reproduction or distribution.

Exceptions to this rule include brief quotations that may be incorporated into critical reviews, as well as certain other noncommercial uses that are allowed by copyright law. Any such usage must adhere to the specified conditions and permissions outlined by the copyright holder.

Note publishing by 402 Creative LLC

DEDICATION

First and foremost, I give honor to God—and a special, most honorable mention to the Holy Spirit, our Advocate, our Helper. The One who dwells within us, guiding us, empowering us to walk boldly in our God-given purpose. None of this would be possible without You.

To my children—Liam, Rylie, Sophie, Teigan, and any future little ones not yet earthside—you are my inspiration. You taught me what love truly is. You gave me purpose, and for you, I will continue to pour out all that I have. My prayer is that I lay a strong foundation beneath your feet and give you a runway long enough to take flight toward your wildest dreams.

To my husband, Kirk—my best friend and greatest champion. You once told me that you knew we were destined to do something amazing together from the moment we met. You had no idea it would be *this* amazing. And yet, here we are—still building, dreaming, and doing. Thank you for believing in me, loving me, and standing beside me through it all. I know God sent you to be my anchor. Just look at us now.

CONTENTS

Introduction ---------------------------------- 5
Chapter 1. Practice Gratitude ------------------- 8
Chapter 2. Educate Yourself – Be a Good Student -- 15
Chapter 3. Aliment – Nourish Yourself ----------- 22
Chapter 4. Compassion – Be Generous ------------- 29
Chapter 5. Empower Others (Give Back) ----------- 36
Resources ------------------------------------ 50
About the Author ----------------------------- 51

INTRODUCTION

The road to peace wasn't one I planned to travel—it wasn't even a road I knew I needed to be on until life presented me with a series of unexpected challenges that forced me to face it head-on. From going from zero kids to three in just three years—without any multiple births—to the sudden loss of a job I had devoted my entire adult career to, and then the heartbreaking, untimely passing of my dad, life felt like it was coming at me all at once. As a daughter who was incredibly close to my dad, this was a loss I could hardly comprehend.

My mental health should have been shattered—overwhelm, anxiety, and exhaustion were knocking at my door, ready to claim me. Have you ever experienced so many unexpected turns in your life that it feels like everything is spinning out of control? For me, it was like juggling too many plates. The more I tried to balance, the more I felt like something would eventually break.

But I knew I had to make a change.

People would ask me how I managed it all—three under-three kids, a demanding new job in technology, and the weight of everything else—and I would simply answer, "Prayers and tears." Prayer was something I had been taught as a child, even though I wasn't living out my faith at the time. Yet, I leaned into it more than ever before. It was through these prayers, and honestly, a lot of tears, that I began to find my footing again.

Then one day, a colleague asked me something that stuck with me: "How do you do it all? How do you come in here daily, handle the chaos at home, and still encourage us to be our best?" And in that moment, I realized that I had stumbled upon a formula, a framework that not only helped me survive but thrive in the midst of challenges. And so, *The Journey to Perfect*

Peace was born.

I began to shift my mindset and the posture of my heart, consciously choosing to see the positive rather than focusing on the drain. The first steps—practicing gratitude, being a curious student, showing generosity, and nourishing myself holistically—became the foundation of the program I now share with others.

But was it easy? No, not at all. There were moments of doubt, times when I questioned whether it was worth continuing or whether I should just fall back into old, comfortable habits. But every time, I kept my eyes on the bigger picture: What would happen if I stayed the course? How would my life, my family's life, and my peace transform if I truly committed to this path?

Then something profound happened: I had a shift. I began to realize I wasn't just surviving anymore. I was living in a place of surrender—not giving up, but giving in to the leadership of God in my life. Once I saw how dramatically my life had changed, I knew I couldn't keep the lessons and tools I'd learned to myself.

Before we start talking about what *perfect peace* is, let's establish what it is *not*. It is not a reality where there is no struggle or issues. That just does not exist. You will always have challenges to face and obstacles to overcome. That's the beauty of growth. The beauty of Perfect Peace is that as you face these challenges and obstacles, you don't carry stress or anxiety because you know there will always be a way through. Peace is being able to approach life and all its curveballs with a smile.

So, I created a program that teaches others how to develop emotional intelligence, spiritual awareness, and overcome self-doubt, confusion, and overwhelm. This program evolved over the years but has always remained centered around the core concepts of mindset transformation, purpose alignment, and living a life of obedience. It is a framework that has helped people pivot toward their purpose, discern the voice of God, and open doors through obedience.

Whenever I see someone else experience the same transformation I underwent, my heart is full of joy. This journey is not just about personal peace—it's about helping you uncover your purpose, trust your path, and ultimately live the life you were meant to live.

CHAPTER 1:
PRACTICE GRATITUDE

I had three kids in three years. That's not a humblebrag—it's a reality that nearly brought me to my knees. The sleep deprivation, the constant demands, the noise, the chaos... it took a toll. And in the middle of it all, I still had to show up to work, engage in meetings, smile, and pretend I wasn't living on fumes.

I remember one particular engagement meeting at work where we were asked to share our biggest fear as an icebreaker. The idea was to practice vulnerability, which sounds great in theory. When it was my turn, I said my biggest fear was not being able to raise my children to completion—meaning, either they or I might leave this world too soon.

The room fell silent. No one really understood the weight of what I said—except one person. One other parent in the room nodded with quiet understanding. Everyone else gave polite smiles or looked confused. For them, it was a stretch. For me, it was my reality. When you've got three tiny humans depending on you for everything, the thought of not being there—of not finishing what you started—haunts you.

A few months later, nothing had really changed on the surface. The sleepless nights were still happening—some worse than others. I vividly remember one night that nearly broke me. Both my daughters, 1.5 years old and 5 months, were having a rough time. They just wouldn't settle. I had one hand in the crib and the other in the toddler bed, rubbing their bellies, trying anything to soothe them. It was 3 a.m., and I was praying that my son, the oldest at just three years old, wouldn't wake up sick because I had officially run out of hands, out of energy, out of patience.

I was completely overwhelmed. Exhausted. Frustrated beyond belief. I felt like I was hanging on by a thread.

That night stayed with me, but not for the reason I expected.

I walked into work the following week and immediately sensed something was off. The air was heavy. People were quiet, somber, like something terrible had happened, but no one wanted to speak it out loud.

My manager eventually pulled me aside into a private office. And then came the news that knocked the wind out of me: the colleague-the one other parent in that meeting—had just lost their oldest child. He was only eight years old.

It rocked me to my core. I felt gutted. And then something inside me shifted—instantly.

All the things I had been complaining about, the exhaustion, the sleepless nights, the endless demands... suddenly, they weren't burdens. They were blessings. I wasn't stuck with what I *had* to do—I was privileged by what I *got* to do.

I *got* to hold my babies through the night.

I *got* to be there when they cried.

I *got* to hear their laughter and their whining, clean up their spills, and break up their toddler fights.

I got to be their mother.

That perspective shift didn't erase the hard stuff but reframed it. Gratitude became my anchor. It was the lens that changed everything. From then on, I committed to finding something, anything, to be grateful for, even in the messiest, most exhausting moments.

Because of the alternative? The unthinkable alternative that one parent in that meeting had to face? It made me realize how sacred even the struggle could be.

Gratitude is not about pretending things are perfect. It's about honoring what *is*. It's about shifting our mindset from scarcity to abundance, from frustration to appreciation. It doesn't make the hard times disappear, but transforms how we carry them.

And in that transformation, we find a new kind of strength.

> *"Make thankfulness your sacrifice to God, and keep the vows you made to the Most High."*
> **– Psalms 50:14 NLT**

Gratitude is more than just a polite "thank you" or an occasional nod to the good things in life. It is a profound emotion, one that holds the power to transform your perspective and bring lasting peace. When we practice gratitude, we shift our focus from what we lack to what we have, and this simple yet powerful shift is the cornerstone of emotional and spiritual well-being.

In our fast-paced world, it's easy to overlook the small blessings we receive daily. We get caught up in what's wrong, in what's missing, or in what's ahead of us. But gratitude invites us to pause, reflect, and truly appreciate the present moment. It asks us to recognize that, despite challenges, there is much to be thankful for. This awareness, this act of seeing the good around us, is the first step toward cultivating peace.

The Power of Gratitude

Gratitude is not just a nice sentiment but a practice that holds tangible benefits for our mental, emotional, and physical health. Studies have shown that people who consistently practice gratitude experience lower stress levels, better sleep, improved heart health, and a greater sense of happiness. But the benefits don't stop there. Gratitude leads to a host of positive emotional and psychological outcomes, including:

- **Selflessness**: Grateful people often feel compelled to give back, to serve others, and to offer kindness. This selfless spirit nurtures deeper connections and strengthens our sense of community.

- **Increased Awareness**: Being thankful sharpens our awareness of the blessings in our lives, from the biggest to the smallest, fostering a sense of appreciation that spills over into all areas of life.

- **Compassion**: Gratitude softens our hearts and makes us more empathetic toward others, recognizing that we are all interconnected.

- **Purpose**: When we are thankful, we acknowledge that our lives have meaning, that there is a higher purpose to our existence, and that our journey is guided by something greater than ourselves.

- **Loss of Entitlement**: Gratitude diminishes the sense of entitlement that often leads to dissatisfaction. When we practice gratitude, we shift our mindset from "I deserve this" to "I am thankful for this."

At its core, gratitude is a mindset. It's a way of looking at the world that allows us to see with new eyes. It's a filter that makes it difficult to feel frustrated or agitated when we are actively searching for things to be thankful for. In fact, the more we practice gratitude, the less room there is for negative emotions to take root. The shift in perspective is profound—gratitude is the antidote to stress, bitterness, and impatience. It clears the space for peace to settle into our hearts.

Gratitude is a process. It requires more than just words; it requires an intentional shift in the posture of our hearts. Are we ready to be thankful? Are we open to receiving peace through gratefulness? The heart is where peace begins, and gratitude is the gateway.

When we allow gratitude to take root in our hearts, we make space for peace. The more we express appreciation for what we have, the more we invite calm and contentment to settle in. It's a powerful spiritual practice that requires ongoing reflection and intention. But the rewards are immeasurable: inner peace, a deeper connection to God, and a clearer sense of purpose.

The question is, are we ready to make the necessary adjustments to our hearts? Are we willing to put in the work of cultivating gratitude on a daily basis? If we can answer "yes" to these questions, then we are positioned for true peace.

The journey toward peace doesn't just happen overnight. It's a daily commitment, a choice we make with every breath we take. If gratitude is to become a part of your life, it requires action—real, deliberate action. Below are a few exercises that will help you put gratitude into practice and lay the foundation for lasting peace.

Activity 1:
The Gratitude List

Start by writing down 25 things that you are truly grateful for in your life. It might seem like a lot initially, but I challenge you to dig deep. Think about the things that might seem small or mundane, yet are gifts nonetheless: the ability to see, walk, and laugh. Be thankful for the people who support you, the experiences that have shaped you, and the simple pleasures that bring joy.

Next, write down 25 things that you don't yet have, but believe you will be thankful for one day. These might include goals you're working toward, relationships you hope to cultivate, or personal growth you aspire to achieve. This is where hope and faith come into play. Faith requires us to believe in things we can't yet see, and gratitude for those future blessings strengthens that faith.

> *Tip: If 25 seems like a daunting number, start simple. Be grateful for the air you breathe, the food on your table, or the fact that you can wake up and try again each day. The goal is to build a foundation of thankfulness that opens the door to greater peace.*

The Path to Peace

Peace is not something that comes easily or automatically. It is cultivated, nurtured, and sustained. Practicing gratitude is the first step on this path. It requires intention, effort, and consistency, but the reward is worth it: a life of contentment, joy, and a deep sense of peace that transcends circumstances.

Gratitude is the beginning of peace because it shifts how we see ourselves, others, and God. It removes the obstacles of negativity, entitlement, and discontent, making room for joy, love, and compassion to grow. And when we choose gratitude, we choose peace.

So, take a moment today—right now—and give thanks. You are already positioned for peace. It starts with a simple choice: to be grateful.

Declaration of Gratitude

I choose gratitude as the foundation of my peace. Today, I shift my focus from what I lack to the blessings I have. I am thankful for the people, experiences, and lessons that have shaped me, and I embrace the beauty in both the big and small moments.

I release negativity and entitlement, and open my heart to the abundance around me. I commit to practicing gratitude daily, knowing it invites peace into my life.

Today, I choose gratitude, and in doing so, I choose peace.

CHAPTER 2:

EDUCATE YOURSELF – BE A GOOD STUDENT

Sometimes when I think back to those early parenting years, I can't help but laugh. The sheer amount of patience it required was next level. If I didn't take time to reset—mentally, emotionally, spiritually—I probably would've lost it more times than I can count. It was a lot of challenges, emotional swings, and a constant stream of expectations... it was a lot. And there's no manual for it. You just figure it out as you go; if you're paying attention, life becomes the best teacher.

One lesson came to me on an ordinary morning during my commute to work. I had a friend riding shotgun, and we were making our way through the Bronx, where traffic can feel like a full-contact sport. Out of nowhere, an 18-wheeler cut me off. My friend immediately launched into a full-blown fit of road rage—yelling, throwing her hands up, completely losing it. Meanwhile, I just kept singing along with the music like nothing happened.

She looked at me like I was an alien and asked, "How did that not make you angry?!"

I smiled and said, "Listen, everything isn't a personal attack. Maybe he was in a rush, maybe he didn't see me... either way, no harm, no foul."

She couldn't wrap her head around it, but in that moment, I realized how much I had learned to choose peace over chaos. It wasn't that I didn't feel things—it's that I had started to ask better questions. What if there's another explanation? What if it's not about me at all?

There are always alternative scenarios, always different motives behind people's actions. Life has taught me that it's wiser to focus on solutions and assume positive intent rather than dwell on problems and jump to negative conclusions.

That mindset didn't come overnight. It came from being a student of life. From reading, reflecting, failing, learning, and trying again. From watching how people react and choosing how I want to respond. The more I paid attention, the more I realized that we're always being taught by our kids, coworkers, and even careless truck drivers.

Life is the classroom. We just have to be willing to learn.

> *"How much better to get wisdom than gold! To get understanding is to be chosen rather than silver."*
> **– Proverbs 16:16 ESV**

If you've ever thought that the moment you graduated from school, your days as a student were over, I invite you to broaden your perspective. Being a good student isn't confined to the walls of a classroom or the confines of an academic schedule. In fact, one could argue that the real learning begins after the diploma is handed over. Life itself is the ultimate classroom, and it offers endless lessons to those who are eager, curious, and attentive enough to learn.

The key to perfect peace isn't found in avoiding life's challenges. It's found in how we approach them. How we respond to the unexpected moments—like a frustrating delay in your morning routine—can make all the difference between chaos and calm. A good student seeks out lessons in every experience, even the ones that initially seem inconvenient or uncomfortable.

Let's take a closer look at what it means to be a good student on this journey to perfect peace. How can we equip ourselves with wisdom and understanding in every situation we encounter? It starts with cultivating a mindset of learning. Whether you're in a meeting at work, stuck in traffic, or simply navigating the complexities of personal relationships, you are constantly in a position to learn.

A learning environment is not limited to a physical space with desks and textbooks. Life, in all its richness and complexity, is a classroom of its own. Every moment offers an opportunity to gain insight—if we're open to it. Imagine for a moment that you're heading to work. You've planned your morning carefully: you know how long it takes to get there, and you're on track to arrive early. But then, something unexpected happens.

You decide to stop for coffee, a small indulgence that you normally enjoy before your day begins. Grabbing your coffee typically takes a minute, so you're confident you have enough time. But today, the line is longer than usual. The person in front of you is paying with coins, slowing everything down. You check your watch—now you're running behind.

In this moment, you have a choice: you can allow frustration to overtake you or seek the lesson. Being a good student in life means looking beyond the surface and finding valuable lessons even in these small interruptions. What can you learn from this delay? Perhaps it's the importance of accounting for the unexpected. Maybe you realize that your morning coffee is important enough that you need to build in a little extra time for these types of setbacks. Or maybe, just maybe, this moment offers an opportunity to be generous—to pay for the coffee of the person in front of you and turn what could have been a frustrating delay into a moment of kindness.

In this scenario, the lesson isn't just about coffee or timing. It's about the bigger picture: learning to regulate your emotions, choosing how you respond to life's challenges, and cultivating peace in the midst of potential frustration. This is what being a good student looks like—a willingness to learn from every situation, no matter how trivial it may seem.

Being a good student means actively seeking lessons in everything you do. But how can you develop this mindset? It starts with adopting certain attitudes and practices that make you more open to learning.

- **Be Eager to Learn**

A good student approaches life with eagerness. This doesn't mean being overly ambitious or trying to learn everything simultaneously. Instead, it's about having a genuine curiosity and openness to the world around you. Life doesn't always follow a textbook or a predictable schedule, but that's what makes it so rich with lessons.

When you face challenges or frustrations, ask yourself: *What can I learn from this?* The best students are those who approach each experience with the understanding that every moment, whether it's pleasant or difficult, has something to teach.

- **Be Diligent**

Diligence is the key to mastery in any area of life. It's easy to give up when things get tough, but the good student knows that true wisdom requires perseverance. Whether you're working on a project, managing a relationship, or dealing with personal struggles, diligence helps you stay focused on the goal, even when the path seems challenging.

Perfect peace comes from knowing that no challenge is too great to overcome. You may not always succeed on the first try, but the diligent student continues to learn and grow, refining their approach until they reach their desired outcome.

- **Seek Solutions**

A good student doesn't just focus on the problem; they focus on finding solutions. Life will always present challenges, but the ability to approach these challenges with a solution-oriented mindset is what sets the good student apart. When things go wrong, ask yourself: *How can I solve this? What can I do differently next time?*

By focusing on solutions instead of dwelling on problems, you empower yourself to maintain peace even in the most stressful situations. It's all about mindset. A good student sees obstacles as opportunities to improve and grow.

- **Build Relationships and Seek Feedback**

A good student understands that they don't have all the answers—and that's okay. The best students are those who build relationships and seek feedback from others. Feedback is a vital tool for growth. Whether it's from a mentor, a colleague, or a close friend, constructive feedback helps you see blind spots you might otherwise miss.

But receiving feedback is only one part of the equation. Being a good student also means being willing to give feedback to others in a loving, constructive manner. Relationships are essential to the learning process, and by fostering strong connections with those around you, you create a community of growth and support.

- **Think Ahead**

A good student thinks ahead. They understand that every action has consequences and that planning ahead can save time, effort, and unnecessary stress. When you're navigating life's many decisions, think about the long-term effects of your choices. Will this decision bring me closer to peace or create more chaos? A good student learns to consider their behavior's outcomes before acting.

Thinking ahead isn't about being overly cautious or fearful of making mistakes—it's about being mindful of how your actions will impact your future. Whether it's choosing a career path, making a financial decision, or deciding how to respond in an emotional situation, thinking ahead helps you move forward with clarity and confidence.

Being a good student on the journey to perfect peace requires commitment, patience, and an openness to learning in every moment. It means taking life's challenges as opportunities to grow and improve, seeking wisdom above all else. When you approach life with the mindset of a good student, you begin to see the world through a lens of possibility, understanding that every experience, good or bad, is an opportunity to deepen your peace.

So, step into life's classroom with eagerness and diligence. Seek the lessons in every situation. Build relationships and seek feedback. Think ahead and choose your actions carefully. Above all, remember that perfect peace comes not from avoiding life's challenges, but from learning to respond to them with wisdom and grace.

As you continue on this journey, know that you are not alone. We are all students in this great classroom of life, learning from one another and growing together. And in the end, we will all find the peace we seek—because we have learned how to walk through life's challenges with calm, grace, and understanding.

Declaration of a Good Student

Being a good student is not just about acquiring knowledge—it's about embodying wisdom, understanding, and a peaceful mindset in every area of life. It's about knowing that challenges are a natural part of the journey, but they don't define us. How we respond to those challenges is what truly matters.

So, I encourage you to declare with me:

I am a good student. I learned how to have perfect peace. I learned how to smile at life's challenges. I learned how to overcome. I am a good student.

As a good student, you will continuously seek growth, understanding, and peace, no matter what life throws your way. And in doing so, you will find that perfect peace is not a destination—it is a way of living.

CHAPTER 3:
ALIMENT – NOURISH YOURSELF

At one point, I was binge-watching all the wrong things. Cop shows were my thing, and *Criminal Minds*? Top tier. I don't think I ever missed an episode. But somewhere along the way, I started noticing how it was shaping the way I saw the world—and not in a good way.

One night, I was sitting in my car outside a deli just a block from my house when a man knocked on my window. I cracked it slightly, cautious. He explained that he and his mother were stranded just down the road, their gas tank was on empty, and he asked if I could spare anything to help.

Immediately, my mind jumped to the worst-case scenario. *What if he's a serial killer? Or trying to kidnap me?* I didn't help him. I drove away. And that moment stuck with me—not because of what he did, but because of what *I* didn't do. That wasn't like me. But it was a direct reflection of what I'd been feeding my mind.

It made me realize just how much the things we consume—TV, music, social media—shape our thoughts and behaviors. The fear, the suspicion, the anxiety... it wasn't just showing up out of nowhere. I had been feeding it.

It wasn't just *Criminal Minds*. Another show, *Power*, started to mess with my peace too. I found myself questioning things in my own relationship, as if my husband had a double life (he didn't, not even close). But the seeds of doubt and fear were being planted, episode by episode.

That's when I had to step back and say: *Enough*. Our thoughts are powerful, yes—but what's even more powerful is realizing that we get to shape those thoughts. We choose what we feed our minds. We choose what we allow to take root.

That was a game changer for me.

Nourishment isn't just about what we eat. It's about what we watch, what we read, who we follow, and what we listen to. Our minds need just as much care and intention as our bodies do. Because when we feed ourselves garbage—mentally, emotionally, spiritually—it will show.

But when we choose to nourish ourselves with peace, positivity, truth, and love, that's when the real transformation begins.

> *"And the peace of God, which transcends all understanding, will guard your hearts and your minds in Christ Jesus."*
> **– Philippians 4:7**

Have you ever paused to consider how you absorb the world around you? It's an important question, especially regarding our peace of mind and spirit. We often hear the saying, "You are what you eat." It's catchy and simple, but goes much deeper than just food. The truth is, we are the sum total of everything we consume—physically, emotionally, and mentally.

This consumption goes far beyond our meals. What we take in through our eyes, ears, and hearts profoundly impacts our inner peace. Every form of input affects us more than we may realize, from the music we listen to, to the TV shows and movies we watch, to the conversations we engage in. The things we allow to nourish and entertain us shape our thoughts, attitudes, and actions.

Imagine for a moment that you want to get fit and healthy. You're committed to improving your body, but three times a week, you start your day with a dozen donuts for breakfast. It doesn't take a nutritionist to tell you that this plan won't bring the results you're hoping for. The same principle applies when it comes to our mental, emotional, and spiritual health. If you constantly consume media, music, or even engage in conversations that are aggressive, negative, or draining, how can you expect to feel at peace?

I've experienced this first hand. There was a time when, on my way to work, I would listen to high-energy music or news that left me feeling anxious and on edge. The chaos of the world around me crept into my thoughts, and I noticed how it affected my interactions and my ability to stay calm. But everything shifted when I made a conscious decision to change my consumption. Instead of filling my drive with stress-inducing content, I chose to listen to things that encouraged me, uplifted my spirit, and set the tone for my day. The change was remarkable.

When we nourish ourselves with peace-filled content, we begin to see the world through a lens of calmness and clarity. Nourishing ourselves with positivity, encouragement, and wisdom allows us to stay grounded, no matter what life throws our way. Just like we need healthy food for our physical bodies, we need healthy content for our minds and souls.

We often underestimate how much our intake shapes our inner world. Think about it: we can control our physical health by choosing what we eat, and the same goes for our emotional and spiritual health. But how often do we stop to evaluate what we are truly feeding our hearts and minds? What are we listening to, watching, reading, and talking about?

Music, for example, is an incredibly powerful tool. Have you noticed how a certain song can instantly change your mood? A feel-good anthem can lift your spirits, while a sad or angry song can bring you down or make you feel agitated. The same goes for podcasts, news, and social media. If you're constantly consuming negative, divisive content or are filled with anger, it will inevitably begin to reflect in your own thoughts and actions.

The same principle applies to the people we interact with. If you're surrounded by individuals who drain you emotionally, it can be hard to maintain peace. Conversations that are filled with gossip, negativity, or complaints can weigh heavily on your spirit. On the other hand, engaging with people who uplift, encourage, and inspire you can strengthen your sense of calm and peace.

It's essential to remember that what we consume—not just through our mouths but through our eyes and ears—becomes a part of who we are. And if we're seeking perfect peace, we need to make intentional choices about what we allow to enter our minds and hearts.

Activity Part 1: Examine Your Intake

The first step in nourishing yourself for perfect peace is self-reflection. Take a moment to examine what you're consuming. What are the influences in your life right now, and how are they affecting your peace of mind?

Start by writing down answers to these questions:

- What type of music do I listen to regularly?
- What shows or movies do I watch in my free time?
- Who are the people I spend the most time with, and how do I feel after interacting with them?

You might be surprised by what you find. Are there certain types of music or shows that consistently leave you feeling agitated, anxious, or restless? Are there conversations you engage in that drain your energy or bring negativity into your life? These are the areas where you might need to reconsider your intake. Remember, you have the power to choose what you consume.

Once you've identified your current habits, ask yourself: Are these things helping me grow into the person I want to be? Are they contributing to my peace? If not, it may be time to make some changes.

Activity Part 2: Reposition Yourself and Set a New Tone

Now that you've examined what you're consuming, it's time to make some intentional changes. The goal is to reposition yourself so that your daily intake nourishes and strengthens your inner peace.

Here's how you can set a new tone:

- **Start with Praise and Worship**: Before you listen to the music you typically enjoy, try spending just 15 minutes listening to praise and worship songs. These songs have the power to elevate your spirit, fill you with peace, and set a positive tone for your day. Even if you don't consider yourself religious, the uplifting and positive nature of this music can shift your mindset from stress to peace.

- **Shift Your Viewing Habits**: If you tend to indulge in guilty pleasure TV shows or movies that leave you feeling drained or negative, try replacing them with content that inspires and motivates you. Watch a motivational speech, a sermon, or something that encourages growth and positivity. This simple change can have a profound impact on your mental and emotional well-being.

- **Limit Time with Draining People**: We all have people in our lives who can be emotionally draining. It's important to set boundaries with these individuals. While you may not be able to avoid them entirely, you can limit your time spent with them and protect your peace. Surround yourself with people who encourage and uplift you—those who positively influence your life.

- **Increase Your Time with God**: Lastly, take the limits off your time spent with God. Prayer, meditation, and spiritual reflection are powerful tools for nourishing your soul. Make time for these practices every day. The more you fill yourself with divine peace, the more you will radiate that peace to others.

Nourishing yourself is not just about what you eat—it's about what you take in from all aspects of your life. The content you consume, the people you interact with, and the activities you engage in all play a significant role in your inner peace.

If you want to experience perfect peace, you must be intentional about what you allow into your heart and mind. Fill yourself with things that uplift, encourage, and inspire you. Seek out music, shows, and conversations that bring you joy and peace, and distance yourself from those that cause stress or negativity.

As you begin to reposition your intake and set a new tone, you will find that peace comes more easily. The peace of God that transcends understanding will guard your heart and mind, and you'll discover that the more you nourish yourself with positivity and divine influence, the more peace will flow through your life.

Declaration of Nourishment

I nourish myself with peace-filled content. I choose to fill my heart and mind with things that bring me joy, encouragement, and calm. I set a tone of peace in my life and protect my spirit from negativity. I am intentional about what I consume, and I allow the peace of God to fill me and guide me.

CHAPTER 4:

COMPASSION – BE GENEROUS

I've come to learn that generosity shows up best when it's least expected.

It's not always some big, orchestrated moment. Sometimes it's instinctive—a quiet "yes" before your mind even catches up. That's how it happened for me one afternoon at the deli.

I was waiting for a sandwich I ordered, just going about my day, when a young boy came in. He looked like he was maybe in middle school, grabbing some after-school snacks. When he got to the register, the man behind the counter told him he was $1.50 short. The boy paused, looked down at his handful of items, and started trying to figure out what he should put back.

Before I even thought about it, I told the cashier, "Add it to mine."

The boy looked at me and smiled so big it lit up my whole heart. He said thank you in a voice so sincere and surprised, like I had just given him more than snacks, like I'd given him hope.

That moment stuck with me.

It reminded me that generosity doesn't have to be grand to be meaningful. Sometimes it's the little things—the small, quiet acts that no one else sees—that make the biggest difference. A few dollars. A few kind words. A few minutes of listening.

We get so caught up in what we don't have that we forget how much we do. Time. Encouragement. Patience. A moment of calm. All of those things are gifts, and they cost us nothing to give.

That afternoon reminded me that generosity is less about what we give and more about how we give it. With heart. With intention. Without expecting anything in return.

And here's the beautiful part—those small acts ripple. That boy walked out of the deli a little lighter, and I walked out reminded of who I want to be in this world. Not just someone who gets through the day, but someone who leaves it a little better for someone else.

Generosity isn't just something we do—it's who we become. It's a mindset. A way of moving through the world with open hands and an open heart.

Give freely, not because you have everything, but because you know what it feels like to need something, and what a gift it is when someone shows up.

> "And do not forget to do good and to share with others, for with such sacrifices God is pleased."
> **– Hebrews 13:16 NIV**

Energy is reciprocated, and joy is contagious. Have you ever noticed how a simple act of kindness can brighten someone's day? Whether it's holding the door for a stranger or sending a quick message of encouragement to a friend, the act of giving has a ripple effect. When we give, we don't just change the life of the person we're giving to—we also transform our own lives.

Generosity is one of the greatest gifts we can offer both to others and ourselves. In fact, it's not only about material things like money; generosity can be expressed through time, attention, or kindness. It's about showing a willingness to offer more than what's required, freely and without expectation of anything in return. When we give from the heart, we create a flow of energy that comes back to us in unexpected ways. Generosity strengthens our connections with others and cultivates peace in our lives.

But here's the beautiful part: Generosity is a habit we can all cultivate. It's a mindset, an approach to life that we can practice each and every day. Imagine a world where everyone embraced generosity—not just with their wealth, but with their time, energy, and love. The world would be a much warmer, more peaceful place. And the best part? You don't need to be rich or have an abundance to be generous. You only need a willingness to give and a heart that desires to make a positive difference.

While financial generosity is undoubtedly powerful, the most significant acts of generosity often come in free and abundant forms. A smile, a kind word, a helping hand—these are all gifts that require no money, but they have an immeasurable impact. When we choose to be generous with our time, attention, and kindness, we are sowing seeds of peace, love, and goodwill in the world. And as we do so, we often find that the very peace we give away is the peace we receive in return.

Consider the power of a compliment. A simple, sincere compliment can change someone's entire day. It costs nothing, yet the effect can be profound. When was the last time you offered someone a genuine compliment? Not the kind of compliment that feels forced or obligatory, but one that comes from the heart. When we give heartfelt compliments, we acknowledge the worth of others, and in doing so, we contribute to their peace and self-esteem.

The same applies to acts of service. Whether it's running an errand for a neighbor, volunteering at a local shelter, or simply listening attentively when someone needs to talk, these acts may seem small, but they carry immense value. Every time we give a piece of ourselves—whether it's our time, energy, or love—we create an environment where peace and kindness can flourish.

I remember a time when I was going through a particularly tough season in my life. I felt overwhelmed, stressed, and disconnected from the world around me. One afternoon, I decided to visit a local nursing home to volunteer. I didn't know exactly what I would do there, but I felt a strong pull to offer something, anything, to brighten someone's day.

When I arrived, I spent time with an elderly woman named Mrs. Thompson. She was quiet at first, but as we talked, she began to share stories of her life. By the end of my visit, we laughed together, and she held my hand, thanking me for the company. That day, I realized that by giving my time, I had not only brightened her day but I had also received something precious in return: a sense of connection and peace.

Generosity is like a pebble dropped into water—the ripples spread far beyond where the stone first hit. Every generous act, no matter how small, has the potential to affect many others in ways we may never fully understand.

Think about a time when someone was generous to you. Maybe it was a friend who showed up with a meal when you were sick, or a colleague who took the time to encourage you when you were struggling. That act of kindness likely had a lasting impact, didn't it? It may have lifted your spirits in the moment, but it also probably inspired you to do something kind for someone else. That's the beauty of generosity: it creates a cycle of goodwill and compassion.

When you give, you not only help the person you're giving to, but you also set an example for others. Your actions inspire others to act kindly, and before you know it, generosity becomes contagious. This ripple effect has the power to create a culture of peace and compassion, and the world becomes a better place for everyone.

Generosity has the added benefit of strengthening our own sense of peace. When we give from a place of love and compassion, we fill our hearts with gratitude. Gratitude is a powerful force. It shifts our perspective from what we lack to what we have and reminds us that we are all interconnected. The more we give, the more we recognize that we are part of something much bigger than ourselves.

Activity: Brainstorm Ways to Be Generous

Generosity doesn't require a grand gesture. In fact, some of the most impactful acts of generosity are small, everyday acts. To help you focus on practical ways to be generous, take a moment to brainstorm 10 ways you can practice generosity this week. These acts could be anything from donating your time to offering a kind word. Here are a few ideas to get you started:

- Buy coffee/tea for a co-worker or friend.

- Compliment three people sincerely today.
- Smile at a stranger and wish them a great day.
- Pray for a stranger who seems down or out of sorts.
- Offer to help a friend or neighbor with a task they've been struggling with.

Take some time to reflect on these ideas. Is there one or two that you could commit to today? Sometimes, the smallest acts can create the biggest shifts in our lives and the lives of others.

Challenge: 10 Days of Generosity

Generosity is a practice. It's a way of living that requires intention and mindfulness. To help you begin incorporating generosity into your daily routine, I challenge you to commit to 10 days of generosity. Complete one act of generosity from your list above each day, or feel free to add your own unique ideas.

By the end of these 10 days, you will notice how your small acts of kindness ripple out, creating a positive environment around you. You will also find that your own heart begins to overflow with peace and joy. When we give freely, we become more connected to others and more grounded in the peace that generosity brings.

Generosity is a beautiful, powerful force that can transform the world around us. It's not just about what we give but the intention behind our giving. When we give from a place of love, kindness, and peace, we create a ripple effect that spreads far beyond our immediate circle. And in doing so, we also invite peace into our hearts.

So, what can you do today to be generous? It doesn't have to be big, but it should be intentional. Whether it's giving your time, your energy, or a simple smile, each act of generosity brings you closer to the peace you seek.

Remember, when you give, you are not only making someone else's life better but also making your own life better. The more we give, the more we experience the joy, peace, and satisfaction that comes with living a generous life.

Declaration of Generosity

I am generous with my time, my words, and my actions. I give freely, knowing that each act of kindness brings peace and joy. I choose to make the world a better place, one small act of generosity at a time.

CHAPTER 5:

EMPOWER OTHERS – GIVE BACK

There was a guy at my job—Jarvis. I'll always remember him, not just because he was a genuinely kind person, but because he was the first person who made me realize that I had something to give. That I could help people, not with anything fancy, just with perspective.

Jarvis carried a lot of stress. You could see it on his face, his posture, and how he moved through the day. One afternoon, he asked me, "How do you stay so positive with everything going on in the world?" This was back in 2018, and if you remember, that year felt like a nonstop wave of national and global heaviness. There was no shortage of reasons to feel anxious, angry, or overwhelmed.

Instead of answering right away, I asked him a question: "What are you watching? What are you listening to?" He admitted that he had been glued to the news, consuming it like it was a train wreck. Hard to watch, but even harder to turn away from. That hit home. I had been there too.

So I offered him a few pointers. Simple things: be mindful of what you take in, create space for peace, choose your inputs with the same care you'd choose your food. I didn't think much of it at the time—it was just a casual conversation in a hallway.

But a week later, Jarvis came back to me. He looked lighter. He smiled more freely. He said, "I just wanted to thank you. After following your advice, this past week has been the calmest and most at peace I've felt in a long time."

That moment stayed with me. It was the first time I realized that the work I was doing on myself wasn't just for me. It could help others too.

I had stumbled upon something powerful: when you find tools that bring you peace, share them. When you figure out how to shift your mindset, teach someone else. Empowerment doesn't have to be loud or public or perfect—it can be as simple as a conversation in a breakroom that changes someone's day, or even their life.

We're not meant to keep wisdom to ourselves. When you've climbed out of a hole, leave a light behind for the next person. When you've found calm in chaos, speak on it. Your story might be someone else's breakthrough.

That's what it means to empower others—not to have all the answers, but to be willing to share what's helped you along the way.

> *"Keep putting into practice all you learned and received from me—everything you heard from me and saw me doing. Then the God of peace will be with you."*
> **– Philippians 4:9 NLT**

Empowering others is one of the most rewarding practices you can adopt in your journey toward perfect peace. It is a practice that transcends individual satisfaction and extends into the hearts and lives of others. When we empower those around us, we create a ripple effect that influences not only our own lives but also the communities and environments we belong to.

Giving back is not just about financial donations or grand gestures; it's about the energy we pour into others. It's about uplifting those around us with encouragement, knowledge, and support. It's about empowering others to recognize their own potential and helping them see that they, too, can overcome challenges and achieve greatness.

In this chapter, we'll dive into the importance of giving back, empowering others, and how it connects deeply with our journey to find perfect peace. It's about fostering an environment of reciprocity, where the more you give, the more you receive. The impact of empowering others is not just in the act itself, but in how it shapes your own life and mindset.

Many people mistakenly believe that when we are struggling or feeling drained, we should hold back and focus only on ourselves. But what I have learned is that the opposite is often true. The power of reciprocity is greater than we realize. When we offer something to others—whether it's a kind word, a helping hand, or a smile—it returns to us in unexpected ways.

The concept of reciprocity is deeply rooted in human connection. As we engage with others, we enter a cycle of giving and receiving. The energy we put out in the world—whether positive or negative—ultimately circles back to us. The more positive energy we send out, the more positive energy we receive.

I remember a moment at work when a co-worker approached me and asked, "How is it that you're always so energetic and positive, no matter what happens?" It seemed like a simple question, but the underlying meaning was clear:

they were curious about how I maintained my positivity. My response was straightforward: "I'm not always at a 'level 10' with engagement and energy. In fact, I usually come in at a level 5, just like everyone else. But when I pour into you and offer encouragement and support, you all pour so much energy back into me. It's the power of reciprocity."

This exchange taught me something profound: when you pour positivity into others, they, in turn, pour that same positivity back into you. And this doesn't just apply to work—it applies to every aspect of life. Whether it's in relationships, communities, or everyday interactions, the act of giving empowers both the giver and the receiver.

One of the simplest yet most powerful ways to empower others is through encouragement. It costs nothing to offer a kind word or a compliment, but the effects can be life-changing. Think about a time when someone's encouragement made a difference in your life. Maybe it was a mentor who believed in you when you doubted yourself, or a friend who reminded you of your worth when you were feeling low.

Empowering others through encouragement is about helping them see their potential, especially when they can't see it for themselves. Encouragement is about offering a positive perspective, even when life is challenging. It's about being a cheerleader for the people around you, celebrating their victories, and reminding them of their strength in moments of doubt.

I've had my share of moments where I felt overwhelmed or uncertain about my path. In those times, I found myself reaching out to others who could offer words of encouragement. It was during these moments that I truly understood the power of empowering others—by lifting them up, I found that I, too, was lifted. This cycle of mutual encouragement created an environment where everyone felt supported, understood, and empowered to keep moving forward.

Encouraging others is not only a way to give back, but it is also a way to fortify your own peace. When you lift someone else's spirit, you are, in turn, lifting your own. It's a practice of empowerment that works on both sides.

When we give back to others, we create a ripple effect that can change entire communities. The idea of a "ripple effect" is simple: your actions have consequences that extend far beyond your immediate circle. Each positive action you take not only impacts the person you're directly interacting with but also influences everyone they come into contact with.

Imagine this: you smile at a stranger, and in return, they smile at someone else. Maybe the smile sparks a positive interaction with their co-workers or family members. In the same way, when you encourage someone, that person may go on to encourage others. A single act of empowerment creates waves that flow outward, affecting countless people in ways we can't always measure.

This ripple effect is especially powerful when we look at it from the standpoint of the community. In communities where people are encouraged and empowered, the overall energy is positive, and individuals are more likely to help and support one another. Empowerment creates a culture of growth, trust, and peace. It fosters an environment where people feel supported and valued, which in turn creates a sense of peace within the community.

This isn't just a nice idea—it's a reality that we can create by empowering others. When we make the effort to give back, whether through encouragement, acts of service, or simply being there for someone, we are contributing to a larger movement of peace and positivity. This is the power of reciprocity in action.

Practical Ways to Empower Others

Empowering others doesn't require grand gestures or extraordinary effort. It can be as simple as offering your time, attention, or skills. Here are a few practical ways you can empower those around you:

- **Mentorship:** If you have a skill or expertise, offer to mentor someone who is looking to grow in that area. Sharing your knowledge is one of the most empowering things you can do for someone.

- **Support their dreams:** Be a cheerleader for the people around you. Help them set goals and offer guidance when they need it. Sometimes, all someone needs is a little encouragement to realize their potential.

- **Be a good listener:** Sometimes, the best way to empower someone is simply by listening. Let them feel heard and understood. Offering a listening ear can give someone the confidence they need to move forward.

- **Share resources:** If you have knowledge or tools that could help someone, offer them freely. Whether it's advice, connections, or tangible resources, sharing what you have can make a big difference in someone's life.

- **Celebrate others:** When someone achieves something, no matter how small, celebrate it with them. Acknowledge their hard work and encourage them to keep pushing forward.

When you empower others, you also empower yourself. As you pour into the lives of those around you, you begin to feel more connected to them. You start to see the world as a place where everyone has the potential for greatness, and you are a part of that greatness.

As Philippians 4:9 reminds us, "Keep putting into practice all you learned and received from me—everything you heard from me and saw me doing. Then the God of peace will be with you." This is a call to action—put into practice what you have learned. Empower others as you have been empowered. As you do, you will experience the peace that comes from knowing that you are part of a greater, more powerful purpose.

Declaration of Empowerment

I am committed to empowering others. I share my knowledge, my encouragement, and my love freely. I recognize that by lifting others, I am lifting myself. I choose to be a force for positive change, contributing to a world filled with peace, empowerment, and reciprocity.

As we come to the end of this journey toward perfect peace, I want to pause and reflect on the steps we've taken together. Each chapter has been a building block, a piece of the puzzle, guiding us toward a more peaceful life—a life where our hearts are at ease, our minds are calm, and our spirits are aligned with the greater purpose we've been called to fulfill.

We began with **gratitude**, recognizing that peace starts with a mindset shift. When we practice gratitude, we open ourselves to see the blessings surrounding us, regardless of our challenges. It's not just about acknowledging the good things; it's about cultivating a heart that chooses to see, appreciate, and embrace the good, even in difficult moments. Gratitude empowers us to shift our focus from what we lack to what we have, and that simple act of recognition brings peace into our lives.

From there, we moved to **education**, understanding that being a good student in the school of life is vital for growth. Life offers endless lessons, and every moment can be an opportunity to learn. Whether it's how we respond to challenges, manage our time, or navigate relationships, being a diligent learner helps us find peace in the most unexpected places. As we educate ourselves, we increase our capacity to find solutions and remain calm, even when life doesn't go as planned.

Next, we discussed **nourishment**—the importance of what we consume and how it shapes our inner world. We have the power to control what we feed our minds, bodies, and spirits. What we allow to enter our lives through music, media, and conversations has a profound impact on our emotional and mental health. By nourishing ourselves with positive influences, we align our thoughts and actions with peace, creating an environment conducive to serenity and growth.

We then explored **compassion**—how giving back, whether through acts of kindness, words of encouragement, or offering our time, strengthens the fabric of our peace. Compassion is not just about helping others; it's about recognizing the interconnectedness of all human beings. When we give, we receive, and the joy we experience through compassion only amplifies the peace we've cultivated in our hearts.

Empowering others is the next step. We understand that our actions—small or large—can make a significant difference in the lives of others. By sharing our wisdom, energy, and resources, we create a ripple effect that spreads peace worldwide. The act of empowering others does not deplete us; rather, it strengthens us. It reminds us that we are not here just for ourselves, but to uplift those around us, creating a collective peace that transcends individual struggles.

Throughout each chapter, we have built upon the idea that peace is not a passive state but an active choice. Peace requires effort, commitment, and a daily willingness to nurture the practices that lead to a peaceful life. Peace isn't just about the absence of conflict—it's about the presence of something greater: contentment, joy, love, and purpose. Peace is the natural result of living with intention, nurturing your mind and soul, and contributing positively to the world around you.

As you continue on your journey, I encourage you to embrace these practices as part of your daily life. Be a good student in the school of life. Nourish yourself with what brings you peace. Show compassion to others and empower them to do the same. Cultivate gratitude in your heart, for it is the key that unlocks all the doors to peace.

There will be days when challenges arise, and the world may seem overwhelming. But remember this: **perfect peace is a process**—one that requires patience, perseverance, and trust. You've already started this journey, and every small step you take toward peace matters. Don't rush the process. Trust that each action you take, each moment of mindfulness, and each act of kindness is building the peace you seek.

The good news is that peace is not something you need to find—peace is already within you. It's a matter of learning how to cultivate, nourish, and live in alignment with it. When you do this, you will experience peace that transcends all understanding, a peace that will guard your heart and mind.

As Philippians 4:9 reminds us: *"Keep putting into practice all you learned and received from me—everything you heard from me and saw me doing. Then the God of peace will be with you."*

The journey doesn't end here. It's an ongoing, evolving process. But take heart, for with each step, you move closer to the peace that you are destined to live in. Keep practicing gratitude, keep learning, keep nourishing yourself, keep giving, and keep empowering others. In doing so, you will discover that perfect peace was never a distant destination—it was with you all along, waiting for you to embrace it.

Declaration of Peace

I choose peace today. I am a student of life, open to learning and growing. I nourish my mind, body, and spirit with what brings me peace. I give generously, empower others, and seek to build a world of peace. I am thankful for the peace that is already within me, and I choose to live in it every day.

Next Steps:
So, how does all of this play out in real life?

What happens when you actually apply these practical steps to your everyday moments—when you take the tools, the truths, and the mindset shifts and begin to live them out?

Let's be clear: what you've read so far is just the beginning. The journey doesn't end here. In fact, it's only the foundation. But I know it helps to see what this looks like beyond theory. To see the transformation in motion. That's why I wanted to share a real-life before and after—an honest, vulnerable look at what it feels like to walk through this process from start to finish.

I called on one of my most loyal clients and mentees, someone who embraced the work, committed to the journey, and saw powerful results. What stood out to me wasn't just her transformation, but the way she valued the program so deeply that after completing it, she turned around and invested in it again… this time, as a gift for someone else. That's the kind of impact we're talking about.

I believe authenticity is a superpower, so instead of telling her story, I will let her share it in her own words—from the beginning, through the challenges, and into the breakthrough.

Before *Journey to Perfect Peace*, I wasn't lost from God—I was in the process of rebuilding my relationship with Him—but I was lost when it came to rebuilding *me*. I had no clear roadmap. I didn't know what to do first, what to prioritize, or how to put the broken pieces back together in a way that made sense. But in His grace, God sent me a mentor. A guide. Someone to walk beside me as I took the first real steps toward a life where He was not only present, but at the center of it all.

From the very beginning of the course, it was clear this wasn't just another program. This was spirit-led. The Holy Spirit met me in every assignment, lovingly but directly confronting the lies on which I had built my identity. I had been walking around carrying false beliefs about who I was, what I deserved, and what was possible for me. But little by little, those lies started to fall away.

One of the biggest revelations? That *joy is my portion*. Not something reserved for other people who "have it all together." Not a reward for perfection. Joy is a fruit of the Spirit—and it was already mine. I stopped resenting people who seemed effortlessly joyful and started realizing: joy is a daily decision. One I get to make again and again, no matter the circumstances.

I also learned how to hear from God clearly. Not just in moments of desperation, but consistently. I stopped approaching the Bible as a checklist and started reading with hunger—reading for *revelation*, not routine. I learned what it means to obey, even when it's uncomfortable, even when it costs something, even when it stretches me.

What surprised me most is how the lessons didn't end when the course did. They're still with me. Still unfolding. There were things I couldn't fully grasp back then that are now showing up in this season, just when I need them most. That's the beauty of this journey: it plants seeds that keep bearing fruit.

There's one scripture that anchored me throughout the course and continues to echo in my spirit today:

> *"Fear God and obey His commands."*
> **—Ecclesiastes 12:13**

That word hasn't let me go—and I thank God it hasn't.

Journey to Perfect Peace didn't just help me rebuild my life—it helped me rediscover my identity, deepen my faith, and walk boldly in the truth of who God says I am. I'm grateful beyond words. This wasn't just a program. It was a turning point.

Receiving this kind of praise and support is exactly why empowering others has become such a meaningful part of my own journey. To watch someone transform, then turn around and help others do the same—it's a ripple effect that never gets old.

So, what's next?

Let's take it up a level.

If you're ready to build on your newly shifted mindset and take intentional action toward lasting peace, I invite you to join me for the **Mid-Month Gratitude Challenge**, lovingly known as *The Great Reset*.

This 9-day challenge is designed for people who are ready to find a new rhythm and balance in life—one that prioritizes rest, joy, and wisdom. You'll participate in a holistic experience that includes:

- **Biblical strategy** to help you align with God's truth
- **Journal prompts** to reflect deeply and honestly
- **Gratitude assignments** that rewire your mindset for joy
- **Daily encouragement and prayer** to uplift your spirit
- **Physical movement** to reconnect with your body

This isn't just another challenge. It's a reset. A moment to pause, re-center, and remember what truly matters.

When you walk away from this challenge, you'll have more than inspiration—you'll have transformation. You'll develop habits that support the lifestyle you're building. You'll feel refreshed and equipped to face old problems with new clarity. And most importantly, you'll walk away with a personalized plan for how your body and soul can experience rest and joy in your everyday life.

You can join us by registering here

Empower Others – Give Back

You've come this far. You've laid the foundation. Now let's build something lasting—together.

RESOURCES

If you enjoyed this book and found it helpful, check out Okay God, But How? by Tepheret Jones

ABOUT THE AUTHOR

Yahreema McFarlane is the Founder of Dearest Father Ministry and Scripture Strategist Presents:

She is the host of the 2 Steps in the Right Direction Podcast available on Spotify

Yahreema has dedicated her life's work to helping people navigate their seasons of challenge to find the path to purpose and peace.

She has a passion for writing and a knack for teaching and has taken her love for public speaking to Summit Stages across the nation.

www.ingramcontent.com/pod-product-compliance
Lightning Source LLC
Chambersburg PA
CBHW071224070526
44584CB00019B/3140